DISTRESSED

Other Works by Sandy Krolick

Вероника: Сибирская Сказка (Novel)
Veronika: The Siberian's Tale (Novel)
The Recovery of Ecstasy: Notebooks from Siberia
Apocalypse of Barbarians: Inquisitions on Empire
Conversations On A Country Path
Gandhi in the Postmodern Age
Recollective Resolve (On Time and Myth)
Ethical Decision-making Styles
Культурныи критицизм
Myth, Mystery and Magic: Religion in Ancient Egypt
Russian Soul and Collapse of the West
Shambhala (Novel)
Misha (Novel)
On Being and Being Good
Q: Interpreting QAnon
A New Heaven and a New Earth
Philosophic Play
Babel Unhinged
The Siberian Shaman and Western Myth
Notebooks: Philosophical Memoirs
Expelled From The Garden
Agnosis and Parousia
The Strange Case of Donald Trump
On Time's Passage
The Closing of the American Mind

DISTRESSED

SANDY KROLICK

ISLANDS PRESS

NEW YORK : ALTAI KRAI : FLORIDA

ISBN: 979-8-9919579-2-2

Cover art courtesy of
Yuri Ivanov
Altai Krai, Russia

*Wishing only to preserve oneself is
the expression of distress...*

Friedrich Nietzsche, *The Gay Science*

DISTRESSED

IN LIGHT of Donald Trump's recent reelection we must remain vigilant, eyes wide open and cognizant of a distinct sentiment brewing among the more reactionary elements on the Christian Right as they seek to usher in the End Time prophesied in the Apocalypse of Saint John. Within some novel spiritual movements characterizing the troubling direction of a growing flock of New Age faithful, there is the belief that God's Kingdom is already upon us, ushered in by Trump's accession yet again to the pinnacle of American power.

NOT UNLIKE that peculiar form of *distress* afflicting their beloved Apostle Paul (*Thessalonians* 3:1/3:5), the more extreme elements of this New Apostolic Reformation believe they are living in the midst of a foundational spiritual crisis, echoing the sort of torment not unlike what this Apostle experienced awaiting the Second Coming of his Lord and Savior. The basis of this *distress* is a deep-seated despair rooted in the anticipation of a day of reckoning, foreshadowed by the return of their hero to the seat of political power.

GROUPS like the *Kansas City Prophets,* embodying what they proclaim as the dawning of a new Apostolic-Prophetic era, provide a congregational framework operating in lockstep with programs like *Kingdom University,* challenging "believers to shift the mindset of practicing religion into fulfilling God's original Kingdom mandate." This is not unlike statements issuing from *Vanquish Academy* with claims that "God is calling us to advance his kingdom throughout the Earth as never before." Such groups represent only a small sampling of belief systems embodying an eschatological desire for the end of the world as we know it, prophesying the birth of a new heaven and a new earth. It is this sentiment that lies at the root of that existential *distress* motivating these believers' desperate preparation for what they see as groundwork for the final battle.

NOT to put too fine a point on it, in similar fashion, most all of these new apocalyptic cults claim that Trump's ascension once again is a sign that Saint John's revelation is already beginning to manifest itself. At *Life Center Church*, a member of this New Apostolic Reformation — where Elon Musk recently spoke — one of their prophets has claimed that Trump was 'God's choice' to help separate those seeking salvation from the wicked among us. And, of course, those judged wicked would be "thrown into the outer darkness, where there will be weeping and gnashing of teeth" (*Matt.* 8:12).

AGAIN, the nature of the *distress* underlying and afflicting those awaiting this *parousia* has only reinforced their faith concerning Trump's return to power. In this respect, Trump has become a veritable stand-in for Christ himself — their savior now incarnate. Yet such *distress* need not be understood as affecting only the faithful but non-believers as well. The final battle is one that believers see as necessary not only in bringing about God's judgement on disbelievers but essential to ushering in new kingship and a new kingdom on earth. And they believe there will be no room in this new world order for those who lack faith in God or in His chosen representative on earth.

IN POINT OF FACT, recent attempts on Trump's life only serve to reinforce the ungrounded belief widely circulating among the staunchly faithful that he is divinely protected or, more distastefully, that he is the one chosen by God. Of course, he is neither! But, that is not to say the man does not himself have a savior complex. Indeed, he does. But, whether Trump feels himself divinely sanctioned, or is merely playing the part for an ignorant but loyal following, these believers seem willing to submit to his authority; and, in that belief is where Trump's real power lies.

BE THAT AS IT MAY, even after those attempts on his life, Trump still seems unwavering, unfettered, and unleashed from the chains that typically bind us mere mortals. And he appears to be playing out this role in the grandest of fashions. Yet, while he seems to have a savior complex, he is really a born huckster and a con man. Still, it remains to be seen to what extent he will follow through on this charade, if in fact he will be responsive to the *distress* exhibited among his followers, and especially those belonging to these novel apocalyptic movements.

LET'S EXPLORE in some detail the nature of this religious *distress* and how it seems to ground and motivate the curious appeal of Mr. Trump. In reality, *distress* may be seen as foundational to Christian suffering itself — a phenomenon born of the memory of Christ's own suffering on the cross. In a real sense, this is the 'cross' that all Christians must bear. And, perhaps it is in this light that we may understand their view of Trump as 'suffering' for them — on their behalf. And certainly Trump himself promotes this view, that he is their suffering servant.

CHRISTIAN *distress* was born very early on in the history of their faith, in both anticipation and expectation of the return of their crucified savior. Well now, some have projected this belief and expectation unto the most unlikely and unquestionably unfit person, himself rising like a Phoenix from the ashes of defeat only to be resurrected and ascend yet again to the pinnacle of power. Indeed, these religious parallels in the minds of his believers are frightening. And, it is this very *distress* that underlies their faith in the person of a hooligan, a convicted criminal, who by every other measure seeks not only retribution, but self-aggrandizement and self-dealing, the religious trappings apparently a facade, a mere front, as well as an affront to the body politic.

BUT this is very clearly not how the Founding Fathers intended or imagined things to turn out. In point of fact, and as James Madison rightly observed:

> *The aim of a political constitution is, or ought to be, first to obtain for rulers men who possess most wisdom to discern, and most virtue to pursue, the common good of the society, and in the next place, to take the most*

effectual precautions for keeping them virtuous whilst they continue to hold their public trust. (Federalist Papers No. 57)

ONCE AGAIN, 'We The People' have been duped, and have failed in this very assignment described so clearly by Madison. Rather, and by the slightest of majorities — just over one percent of the popular vote — we have succumbed to the very same *distress* informing and enlivening the religiously fearful, the lost, and the prayerful, those who have bent their knee in some vaguely spiritual anticipation and salvific hope against hope. But, it is misplaced hope — born of apocalyptic *distress* — in the likes of an unprincipled man whose principal concern clearly seems to be his own self-glorification and the accretion of more wealth and power.

AS Chris Hedges warned us in his 2007 work entitled *American Fascists:*

> *If these dispossessed were not reincorporated into mainstream society, if they eventually lost all hope of finding good, stable jobs and opportunities for themselves and their children — in short, the promise of a brighter future — the specter of American fascism would beset the nation. This despair, this loss of hope, this denial of a future, [has] led the desperate into the arms of those who promised miracles and dreams of apocalyptic glory.*

AND SO our fears concerning a 'return of the distressed' in such a hot political climate have now been realized through Trump's ascension once again to the seat of power. We have no more excuses, no one to blame but ourselves. The man behind the curtain has stepped forward and is now out at center stage, ready and anxious to perform for our simple amusement and his personal enrichment. And while it has not quite reached *apocalyptic* dimensions, this very moment in history is now seen by believers as signaling the approaching *eschaton* — judgement day — with the reinstallation of their divinely sanctioned mythic hero. Mr. Hedges was perfectly on point when he wrote in *Peace and Planet News,* in the Winter of 2025:

> *We are in the grip of what Soren Kierkegaard called "sickness unto death" — the numbing of the soul by despair that leads to moral and physical debasement. All Trump has to do to establish a naked police state is flip a switch. And he will.*

PERHAPS we have reached the point of no return. Certainly the stage has been set for the makings of a real revolution. After all, on his very first hours in office, and in front of a sea of adoring fans, Mr. Trump pardoned more than 1,500 criminals — all of them convicted felons found guilty of participating in the January 6th insurrection, including the leaders of both the Oath Keepers and the Proud Boys. Even those who had earlier admitted their crimes are not only retracting those confessions, rather they are now promising to be armed and ready for the coming battle. This is more than just an Army of God assembling, my friends; it is, in fact, shaping up to be a genuine Armageddon.

www.ingramcontent.com/pod-product-compliance
Lightning Source LLC
Chambersburg PA
CBHW060551030426
42337CB00021B/4532